Introduction

MSP Principles, tab 3
The purpose of MSP is to provide a co[mmon]
understanding for all programmes. This [is]
principles-based. Principles are characterized as:
- Universal in that they apply to every programme
- Self-validating in that they have been proven in practice
- Empowering because they give practitioners of this framework some added ability to influence and shape transformational change towards success.

MSP Governance Themes, tabs 4-7
Governance Themes provide guidance on concepts that are continual throughout the life of the programme. Most have a cycle of associated activities that enable appropriate controls to be maintained to keep the programme on course.

MSP Transformational Flow, tabs 8-10
MSP programmes are all about delivering transformational business change. The Transformational Flow shows how this transformation is achieved through a series of iterative, interrelated steps. Each process may require more than one iteration before the next one begins.

MSP Programme Information Documents, tabs 11-12
MSP provides guidance on what should be considered when constructing your documentation and when you should review and update the contents. There are three categories of information: boundary information, governance information and management information.

A programme is typically a large investment that should make a significant contribution towards achieving corporate performance targets. A well-managed programme maintains good links with a sometimes volatile corporate strategy.

A programme is a learning organization in that it reflects upon and improves its performance during its life. Good governance requires approaches to managing the different themes that are regularly adjusted and adapted on the basis of experience and results to date.

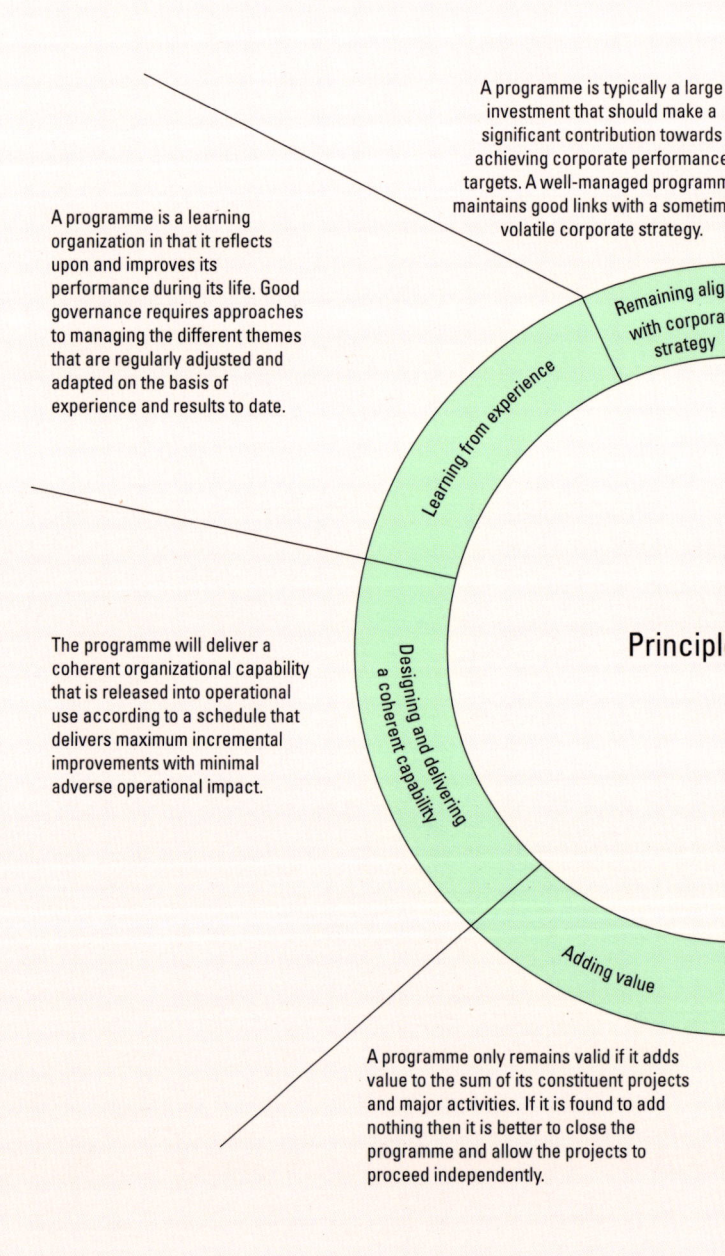

Remaining aligned with corporate strategy

Learning from experience

Designing and delivering a coherent capability

Adding value

Principle

The programme will deliver a coherent organizational capability that is released into operational use according to a schedule that delivers maximum incremental improvements with minimal adverse operational impact.

A programme only remains valid if it adds value to the sum of its constituent projects and major activities. If it is found to add nothing then it is better to close the programme and allow the projects to proceed independently.

Seeing through change in a programme is a leadership challenge. In addition to the need to manage a large number of complex tasks, people have to be led. It is impossible to move to a better future without clear leadership.

Leading change

Envisioning and communicating a better future

A programme is relevant where there is a need to achieve transformational change, where there is some marked step change or break with the present required in the future capability. In order to achieve such a beneficial, future state, the leaders of a programme must first describe a clear vision of that future.

Focusing on the benefits and threats to them

Best practice programme management aligns everything towards satisfying strategic objectives by realizing the end benefits. Thus the programme's boundary, including the projects and activities that become part of the programme, are determined to enable the realization of these end benefits.

Quality & Assurance Mgt

The purpose of quality and assurance management is to ensure that all management aspects of the programme are working appropriately and that it stays on target to achieve its objectives.

Organization

Establishing a clear and effective organization is critical to programme success. Effective programme Organization requires the effective combination of the features: defined roles, clear responsibilities of each of these roles, management structures and reporting arrangements that are needed to deliver the programme's desired outcomes.

Risk & Issue Management

At any point during a programme, there may be events or situations which can affect the direction of the programme, the delivery of its outputs and capability, the achievement of outcomes or the realization of expected benefits. These events or situations are the risks and issues that the programme has to manage and resolve.

Business Case

The senior responsible owner (SRO), the sponsoring group and the Programme Board must have confidence at every stage that the programme is still viable. In MSP the Business Case provides the vital test of the viability of the programme. It answers the question: 'Is the investment in this programme still worth it?'

Planning & Control

Planning and control are key to the success of any transformation programme and should be seen as distinctly separate concepts and activities. Planning involves processing large amounts of information, extensive consultation and building the plan. Control relates to: refine and improve delivery, minimize the impact of ambiguity, bring certainty wherever possible and justify the continuance of the programme.

Governance Themes

Vision

A vision is a picture of a better future. In MSP it is the basis for the outcomes and delivered benefits of the programme. As such, it is a vital focus and enabler for the buy-in, motivation and activity alignment of the large community of stakeholders involved in any programme.

Leadership & Stakeholder Engagement

A stakeholder is an individual or group that can affect, be affected by, or perceive itself to be affected by, a programme. One key aspect of the 'Leading change' programme management principle is that it actively engages stakeholders.

Benefits Management

Programmes are primarily driven by the need to deliver benefits. This is achieved by projects creating outputs, which build capabilities, which transition into outcomes that serve the purpose of realizing benefits for the organization. However, it is likely that the programme will have some negative impacts as well as improvements.

Blueprint Design & Delivery

The programme's Vision Statement provides early and valuable information as a description of the desired outcomes in customer-focused terms. As it is a description at a summary level, it needs to be expanded and developed into a blueprint. It is the blueprint that provides a usable basis for modelling benefits and designing the Projects Dossier.

Programme Organization

Governance Theme

	Sponsoring Group	Programme Board	Senior Responsible Owner (SRO)
Programme organization	The sponsoring group has the overarching authority over the programme. They delegate much of this to the SRO, depending on the nature of the relationship that is established between the SRO and the sponsoring group. **Responsibilities:** – Provides and ensures the continuing organizational context for the programme – Authorizes the Programme Mandate – Authorizes Programme Definition – Participates in end-of-tranche reviews – Approves progression to the next tranche of the programme – Authorizes funding for the programme – Resolves strategic and directional issues between programmes – Authorizes the organization's strategic direction against which the programme is to deliver – Authorizes the progress of the programme against the strategic objectives – Leads by example to implement the values implied by the transformational change – Provides continued commitment and endorsement in support of the programme objectives at executive and communications events – Appoints, advises and supports the SRO – Authorizes the Vision Statement – Authorizes delivery and sign-off at the closure of the programme	Members of the Programme Board are individually answerable to the SRO for their areas of responsibility and delivery within the programme. **Responsibilities:** – Defines the acceptable risk profile and risk thresholds for the programme and its constituent projects – Ensures that the programme delivers within its agreed boundaries. – Resolves strategic and directional issues between projects – Assures the integrity of benefits profiles and the realization plan – Maintains focus on the development, maintenance and achievement of the blueprint – Provides assurance for operational stability and effectiveness through the programme delivery cycle – Provides and commits support to the SRO for the areas that they represent. This may include: – Understands and manages the impact of the change – Monitors the defined benefits achievements – Resolves risks and issues relevant to their area – Resolves dependencies with other pieces of work – Ensures the viability and integrity of the programme blueprint – Represents local strategy as expressed in, e.g. medium-term plans and operational blueprints – Makes resources available for planning and delivery purposes	• Ensures that the programme has the necessary skills, resources and experience required • Puts clear lines of authority in place • Ensures that the sponsoring group members have a clear understanding of their roles • Appoints the Programme Manager. • Approves the BCM appointment
Vision			• Engages the sponsoring group • Produces the Vision Statement doc. • Gains sponsoring group and senior support and commitment for vision • Ensures that the organization is capable of achieving the transformation described • Maintains focus on the vision doc. • Authorizes changes
Leadership and stakeholder engagement			• Engages key stakeholders • Leads the engagement with high-impact stakeholders and anticipates on stakeholder issues that may arise • Briefs the sponsoring group and gathers strategic guidance on changing business drivers • Show visible leadership • Ensures creation, implementation and maintenance of the overall stakeholder engagement strategy
Benefits management			• Reports to the sponsoring group on the delivery of the programme benefits • Ensures that the programme and the business areas affected maintain a focus on benefits delivery • Chairs benefits reviews involving relevant stakeholders, business managers, and possibly internal audit • Liaises with the sponsoring group on the validation of all benefits claimed by the programme • Authorizes benefits achievements
Quality and assurance management			• Ensures an adequate assurance regime • Signs off the quality and information management strategies • Initiates assurance reviews and audits • Maintains focus on the programme management principles

Responsibilities

Business Change Manager(s) (BCM)	Programme Manager	Programme Office
• Designs and appoints the business change team • Inducts and manages the members of the business change team • Develops the individuals of the business change team	• Designs and appoints the programme team • Appoints the Programme Office • Facilitates the appointment of project management teams • Ensures all roles have clearly defined responsibilities • Ensures that the organization design is managed throughout the programme lifecycle • Manages the programme team	• Maintains organization information • Advises on roles and responsibilities within the programme team • Supports in recruitment and appointments
• Supports the SRO in the development of the content • Communicates the Vision Statement • Delivers operational changes	• Develops programme documentation • Ensures that the Vision Statement underpins the programme communications plan • Coordinates the development of the blueprint • Processes changes or updates	• Delivers configuration management
• Engages and leads those operating new working practices through the transition • Generates confidence and buy-in • Alerts the Programme Manager to the net winners and losers • Briefs and liaises with the change team • Communicates with stakeholders to identify new benefits and improved ways of realizing benefits • Delivers key communications messages	• Develops and implements the stakeholder engagement strategy • Develops and maintains the stakeholder profiles • Controls and aligns project communication activities • Ensures effective communications with the project teams • Develops, implements and updates the programme communications plan	• Maintains stakeholder information • Maintains audit trail of communication activities • Collects feedback and ensures that it is logged and processed • Facilitates activities specified in the programme communications plan
• Identifies and quantifies the benefits with support of relevant stakeholders, the Programme Manager and members of the project teams. Develops and maintains benefits profiles • Deliver particular benefits as profiled • Ensures there is no double-counting of benefits • Sets performance deviation levels during realizing benefits	• Develops the benefits management strategy with the BCMs and relevant stakeholders from the affected business areas • Develops the benefits realization plan in consultation with the BCMs and relevant stakeholders and members of the project teams • Ensures delivery of capabilities • Initiates benefit reviews	• Monitors progress of benefits realization against plan • Gathers information for the benefit reviews • Produces performance reports • Maintains benefits information under change control and maintains audit trails of changes
• Implements, transits, realizes and reviews the benefits • Initiates assurance reviews of business performance and change readiness	• Develops and implements the quality and assurance strategy • Plans and coordinates delivery of outputs from the projects • Ensures implementation of lessons	• Establishes and maintains the programme's quality and assurance plan and information management plan • Provides information

Governance Theme

	Sponsoring Group	Programme Board	Senior Responsible Owner (SRO)
Blueprint design and delivery	see previous page for responsibilities		<ul><li>Provides strategic direction</li><li>Ensures sponsoring group authorization and commitment to the 'to-be' state</li><li>Ensures that the blueprint remains aligned with the strategic direction</li><li>Provides interface to sponsoring group and others</li><li>Provides advice and direction to the Programme Manager and BCMs</li></ul>
Planning and control			<ul><li>Consults the sponsoring group and other key stakeholders</li><li>Leads the ongoing monitoring and review activities of the programme</li><li>Monitors progress and direction of the programme at a strategic level and initiates management interventions where necessary</li><li>Authorizes the resource management strategy</li><li>Authorizes the monitoring and control strategy</li><li>Ensures that adequate assurance is designed into the control mechanism</li><li>Authorizes the Projects Dossier, programme plan, and the required monitoring and control activities</li></ul>
Business Case			<ul><li>Accountable for the successful delivery of the programme</li><li>Owns the Business Case</li><li>Secures investment for the programme</li><li>Ensures that the progress of the programme remains aligned to the Business Case</li><li>Ensures the Business Case is monitored, reviewed regularly and updated with more detailed information</li></ul>
Risk and issue management			<ul><li>Authorizes the risk management and issue management strategies</li><li>Intervenes to control risks and issues that affect the alignment of the programme with organizational objectives</li><li>Initiates assurance reviews of risk and issue management effectiveness</li><li>Owns strategic risks and issues</li></ul>

Responsibilities

Business Change Manager(s) (BCM)	Programme Manager	Programme Office
• Leads the development of the content • Takes responsibility for the delivery of the design into business operations • Consults with and gains support from senior business managers for the 'to-be' state • Provides and coordinates essential input, and (where appropriate) authorizes (at least part of) the blueprint	• Ensures the blueprint is authored and assembled • Works closely with the BCMs to ensure that the blueprint, programme plan, benefits realization plan and benefit profiles are consistent and able to deliver the Business Case • Ensures the programme has access to competent resources • Ensures that appropriate appraisal of options takes place to select the optimal 'to-be' state • Contributes to managing stakeholder expectations	• Provides or locates information and resources that can assist • Facilitates impact assessments of changes • Maintains configuration control
• Consults with the Programme Manager on designing the Projects Dossier and scheduling the tranches and constituent projects to ensure the transition will align with required benefits realization • Ensures that changes are implemented in the business • Ensures that the business continues to operate effectively during the period of change • Makes sure operational functions are adequately prepared and ready to change when transition starts • Maintains business operations during the change process until transition and handover is complete • Plans the transition within operational areas	• Designs the Projects Dossier, programme plan, resource management strategy and the required monitoring and control activities • Ensures that the blueprint, programme plan, benefits realization plan and benefit profiles are consistent and able to deliver the Business Case • Develops the resource management strategy and deployment of the plan • Develops the monitoring and control strategy and its deployment • Creates and issues Project Briefs • Identifies and manages programme dependencies • Reports progress to SRO and Programme Board on project, Business Case, programme plan and blueprint achievement	• Supports the development of planning, control and information management arrangements • Gathers information and presents progress reports on projects • Supports the Programme Manager in the development of reports • Provides information and resources that can assist with the design of documentation • Establishes and operates the programme's information and configuration
• Profiles the benefits and dis-benefits and their associated costs • Ensures that benefits continue to be valid • Ensures that the full cost of change is being captured • Controls operational risks to the validity of the Business Case • Measures benefits at the start of the programme and tracks throughout • Manages business change and realization costs • Realizes the profiled benefits	• Prepares the Business Case • Supports the SRO in the ongoing validation and review of the Business Case • Manages the programme's expenditure against the overall investment defined in the Business Case • Identifies opportunities to optimize the Business Case	• Supports the SRO and Programme Manager in compiling and updating the Business Case • Collects and maintains Business Case information • Facilitates Business Case reviews
• Manages and coordinates the resolution of risks relating to operational performance and benefits achievement • Ensures that the risk management cycle includes operational risks • Manages risks that impact on business performance and transition • Identifies operational issues and ensures that they are managed by the programme • Contributes to impact assessments and change control	• Develops and implements the strategies for handling risk and issues • Designs and manages the risk and issue management cycle • Manages the aggregated level of risks and issues. Allocates risks and issues as appropriate • Ensures that change control is undertaken by individuals with the correct authority • Ensures the impact of individual and aggregated risks is understood by the relevant stakeholders • Defines clear rules for escalation, cascade and thresholds	• Manages and coordinates the information and support systems • Maintains the programme Risk and Issue Registers • Establishes, facilitates and maintains the risk and issue management cycle • Provides support and advice on the risks and issues to projects

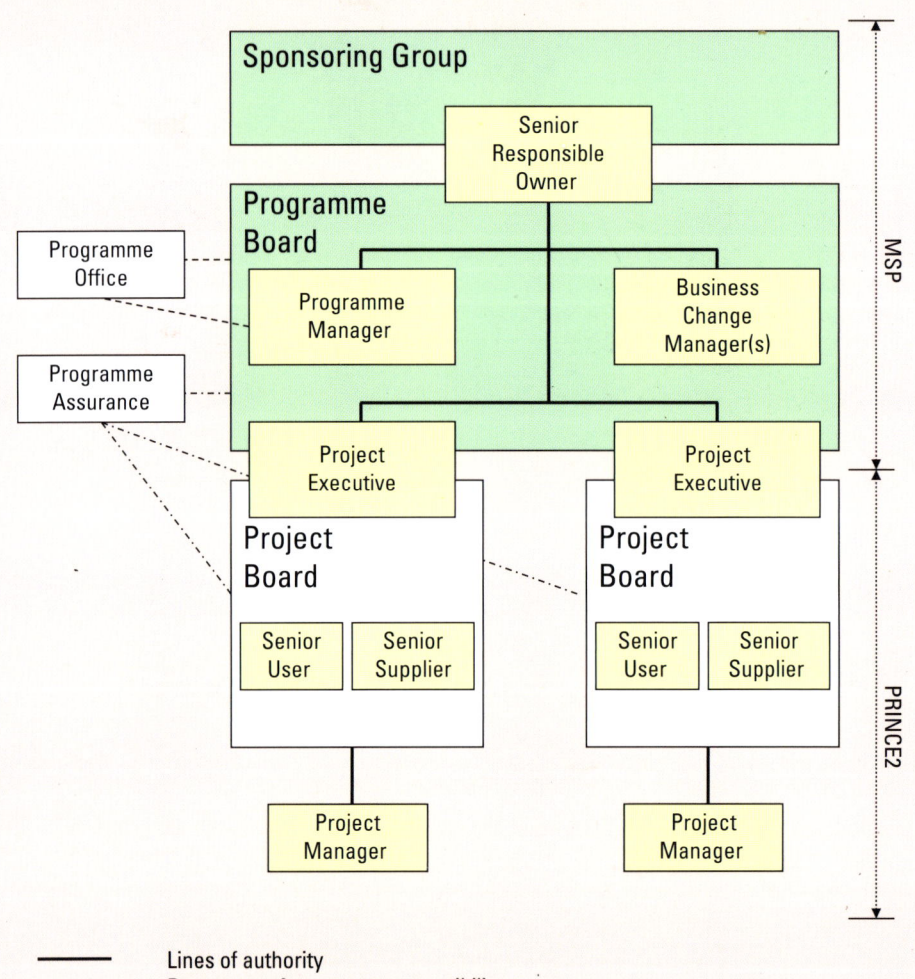

Senior Responsible Owner (SRO)
The single individual with overall responsibility for ensuring that a project or programme meets its objectives and delivers the projected benefits.

Sponsoring Group
The driving force behind a programme, which provides the investment decision and top-level endorsement for the rationale and objectives of the programme.

Programme Board
A group that is established to support an SRO in delivering a programme.

Programme Manager
The role responsible for the set-up, management and delivery of a programme; typically allocated to a single individual.

Business Change Manager(s)
The role responsible for benefits management, from identification through to realization, and for ensuring that the implementation and embedding of the new capabilities are delivered by the projects. Typically allocated to more than one individual and also known as 'Change agent'.

Programme Assurance
Independent assessment and confirmation that the programme as a whole, or any of its aspects, is on track, that it is applying relevant practices and procedures, and that the projects, activities and business rationale remain aligned to the programme's objectives.

Programme Office
The function providing the information hub and standards custodian for a programme and its delivery objectives; could provide support for more than one programme.

Project Executive
The single individual with overall responsibility for ensuring that a project meets its objectives and delivers the projected benefits. The Executive is the chair of the Project Board. The Programme Manager can be the Project Executive for one or more projects.

Identifying a Programme

The concept (corporate strategy, initiative, policy or emerging programme) and the resulting vision that is driving the change generates the Programme Mandate – the trigger for initiating the overall Programme Management process. The signing-off of the programme mandate allows the 'Identifying a Programme' process to begin, where the Programme Brief is developed. 'Identifying a Programme' is typically a short process, perhaps taking only a few weeks or less, which turns the idea into a tangible business concept.

Defining a Programme

Provides the basis for deciding whether to proceed with the programme or not. This is where the detailed definition and planning for the programme is undertaken.

The Programme Brief is used as the starting point for creating the programme definition information.

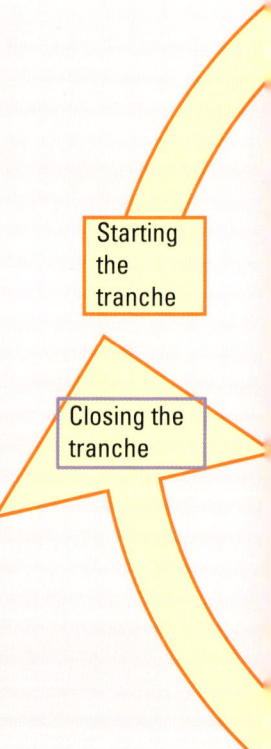

Starting the tranche

Closing the tranche

Delivering the Capability
Covers the activities for coordinating and managing project delivery according to the programme plan. Delivery from the Projects Dossier provides the new outputs that enable the capabilities described in the blueprint. The activities of 'Delivering the Capability' are repeated for each tranche of the programme.

Managing the Tranches
Implements the defined programme management governance strategies for the programme, ensuring that the capability delivery is aligned to the strategic direction of the organization, and enabling the release of benefits. This accepts that, as the programme progresses, it will need to be adapted and refined to assure the effective delivery of the tranches and final outcomes.

Closing a Programme
Programmes tend to last for a significant period, typically, years. There is a danger of allowing the programme to drift on, as if it is part of normal business. The purpose of the 'Closing a Programme' process is to ensure the end goal of formally recognizing that the programme is completed. This is when the programme has delivered the required new capabilities described in the blueprint, and has assessed the outcomes via benefit measures.

Realizing Benefits
Manages the benefits from their initial identification to their successful realization. The activities cover monitoring the progress of the projects to ensure the outputs are fit for purpose and can be integrated into operations such that the benefits can be realized.

MSP Process Purpose

MSP process (every process has its own border color)

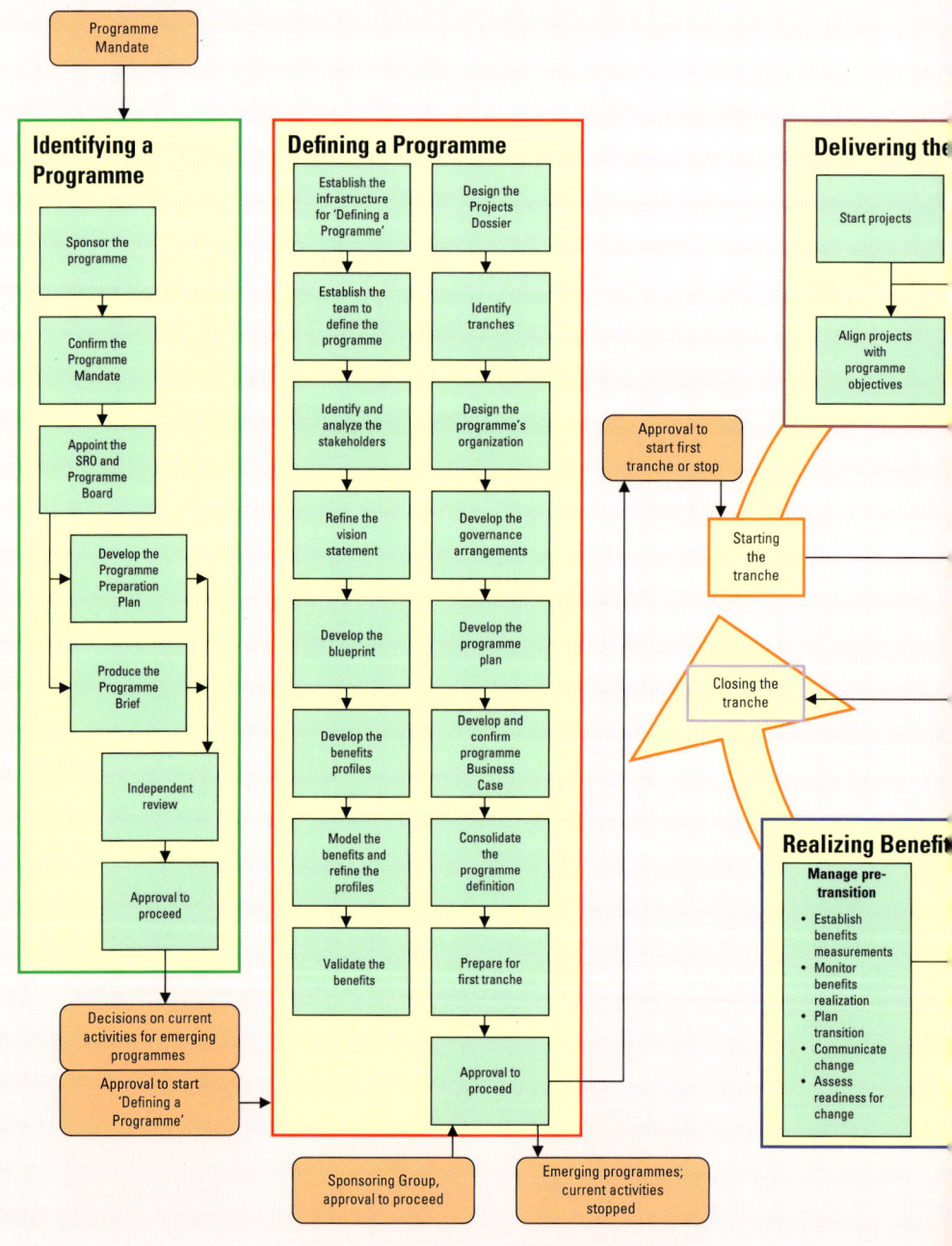

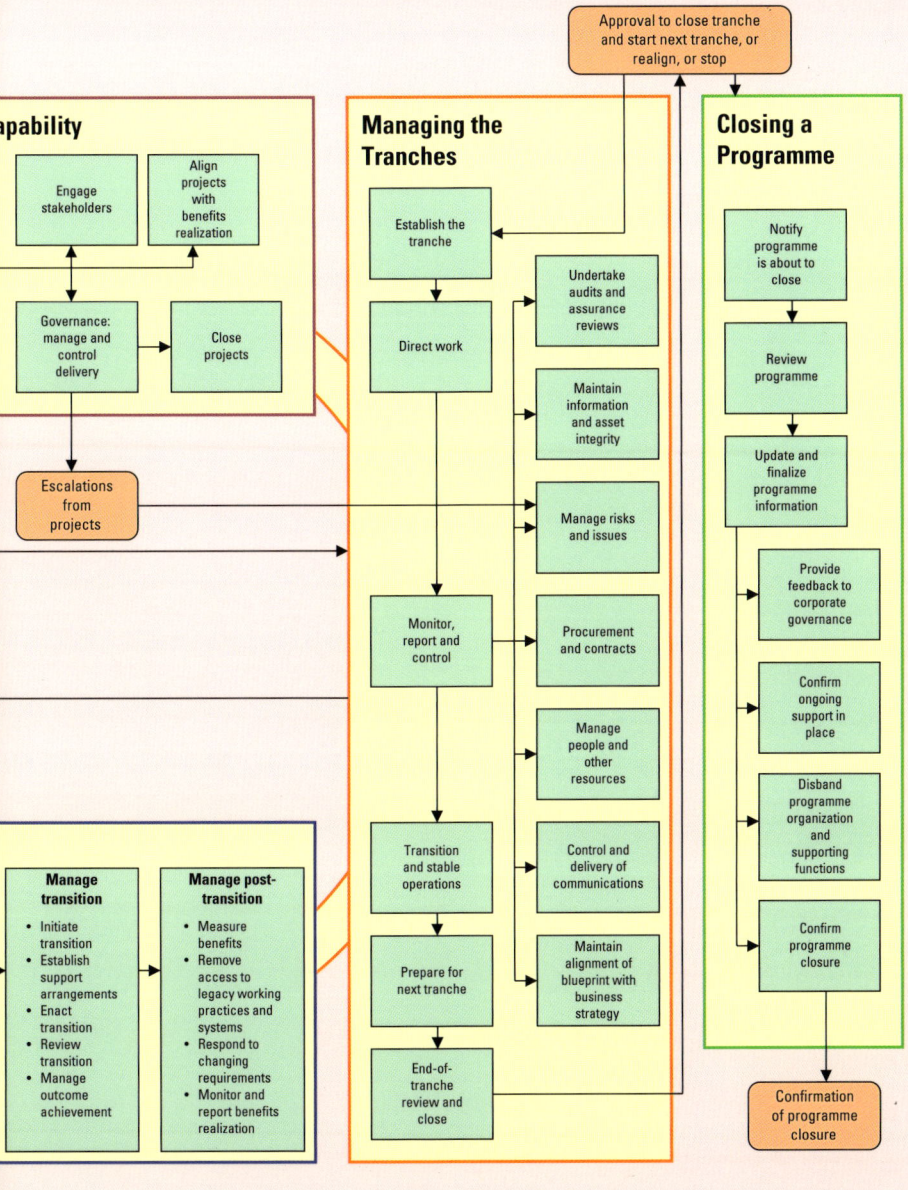

Identifying a Programme

Columns: Sponsoring Group | SRO | Programme Manager | BCMs

Activity	SG	SRO	PM	BCMs
Sponsoring the programme	A			
Confirm the Programme Mandate	A			
Appoint the SRO and Programme Board	A			
Produce the Programme Brief		A	R	R
Develop the programme preparation plan		A	R	R
Independent review		A	R	C	C
Approval to proceed		A	R	C	C

Defining a Programme

Columns: SRO | Programme Manager | BCMs | Programme Office

Activity	SRO	PM	BCMs	PO
Establish the infrastructure for defining a programme	A	R	I	C
Establish the team to define the programme	A	R	I	C
Identify and analyse stakeholders	A	R	C	C
Refine the Vision Statement	A	R	C	
Develop the blueprint	A	R	C	C
Develop the benefit profiles	A	C	R	C
Model the benefits and refine the profiles	A	C	R	C
Validate the benefits	A	C	R	
Design the Projects Dossier	A	R	C	C
Identify tranches	A	R	R	C
Design the Programme Organization	A	R	C	C
Develop the governance arrangements	A	R	C	C
Develop the programme plan	A	R	C	C
Develop and confirm programme Business Case	A	R	C	I
Consolidate the programme definition	A	R	C	C
Prepare for first tranche	A	R	C	C
Approval to proceed	A	R	R	I

Delivering the Capability

- Start projects
- Engage stakeholder
- Align projects with benefits realization
- Align projects with programme objectiv[es]
- Governance: manag[e] and control delivery
- Close projects

Realizing Benefits

Manage pre-transition
- Establish benefits measurements
- Monitor benefits realization
- Plan transition
- Communicate the change
- Assess readiness for change

Manage transition
- Initiate transition
- Establish support arrangements
- Enact transition
- Review transition
- Manage outcome achievement

Manage post-transitio[n]
- Measure benefits
- Remove access to legacy working practices and syste[ms]
- Respond to changin[g] requirements
- Monitor and report benefits realization

R = Responsible (gets the work done)
A = Accountable (answerable for the programme's success)
C = Consulted (supports, has the information or capability required)
I = Informed (notified, but not consulted)

MSP Responsibilities

Managing the Tranches

Activity	SRO	Programme Manager	BCMs	Programme Office
Establish the tranche	A	R	C	C
Direct work	A	R	I	C
Manage risks and issues	A	R	R	C
Control and delivery of communications	A	R	R	C
Undertake audits and assurance reviews	A	R	C	I
Maintain alignment between programme blueprint and business strategic objectives	A	C	R	I
Maintain information and asset integrity	A	R	C	C
Manage people and other resources	A	R	C	C
Procurement and contracts	A	R		
Monitor, report and control	A	R	C	C
Transition and stable operations	A	C	R	C
Prepare for the next tranche	A	R	C	C
End-of-tranche review and close	A	R	C	C

Closing a Programme

Activity	SRO	Programme Manager	BCMs	Programme Office
Confirm on-going support is in place	A	R	C	C
Confirm programme closure	A	C	C	I
Notify programme is about the close	A	R	C	I
Review programme	A	C	R	I
Update and finalize programme information	A	R	C	C
Disband Programme Organization and supporting functions	A	R	I	I
Provide feedback to corporate governance	A	R	C	I

10

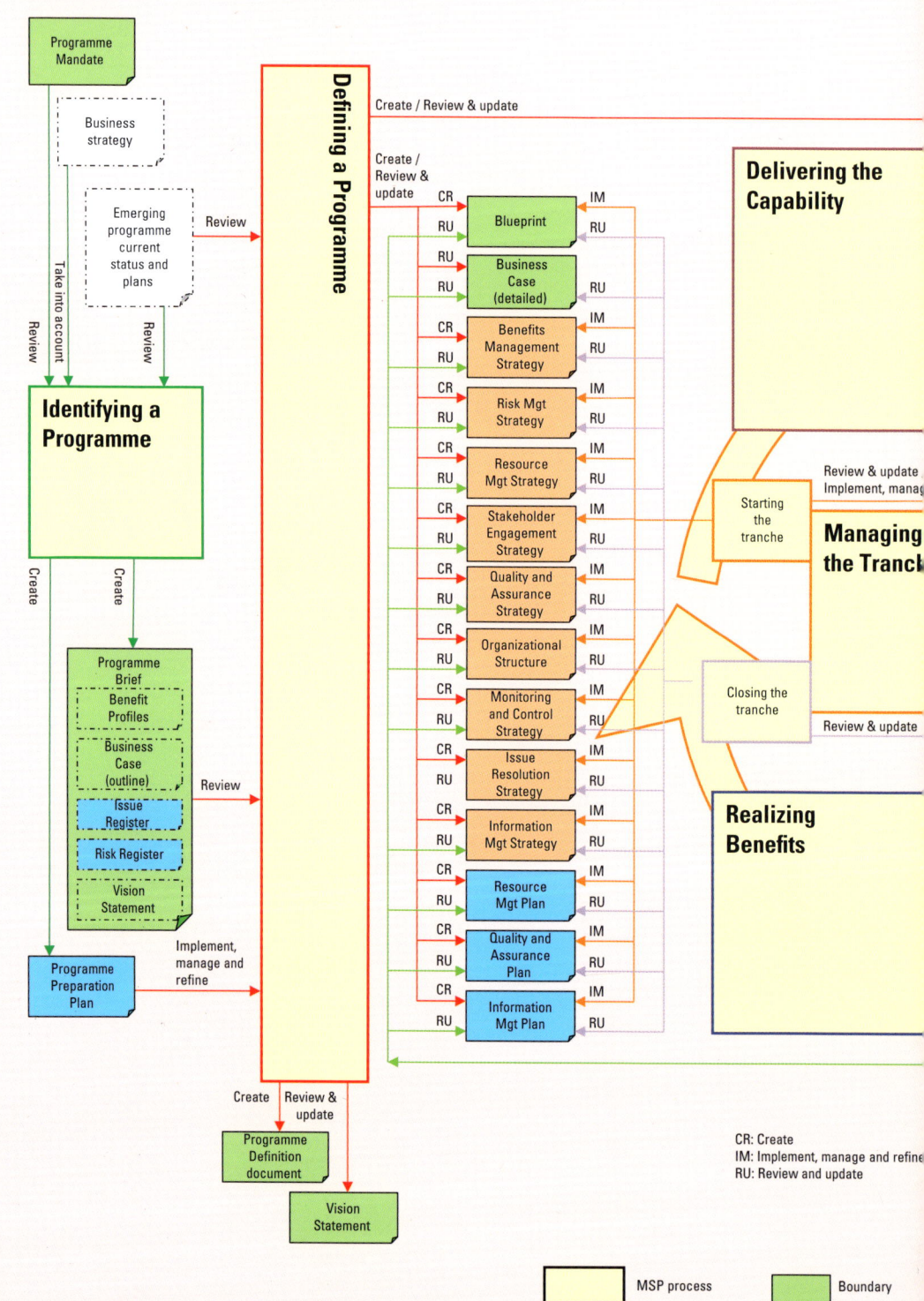

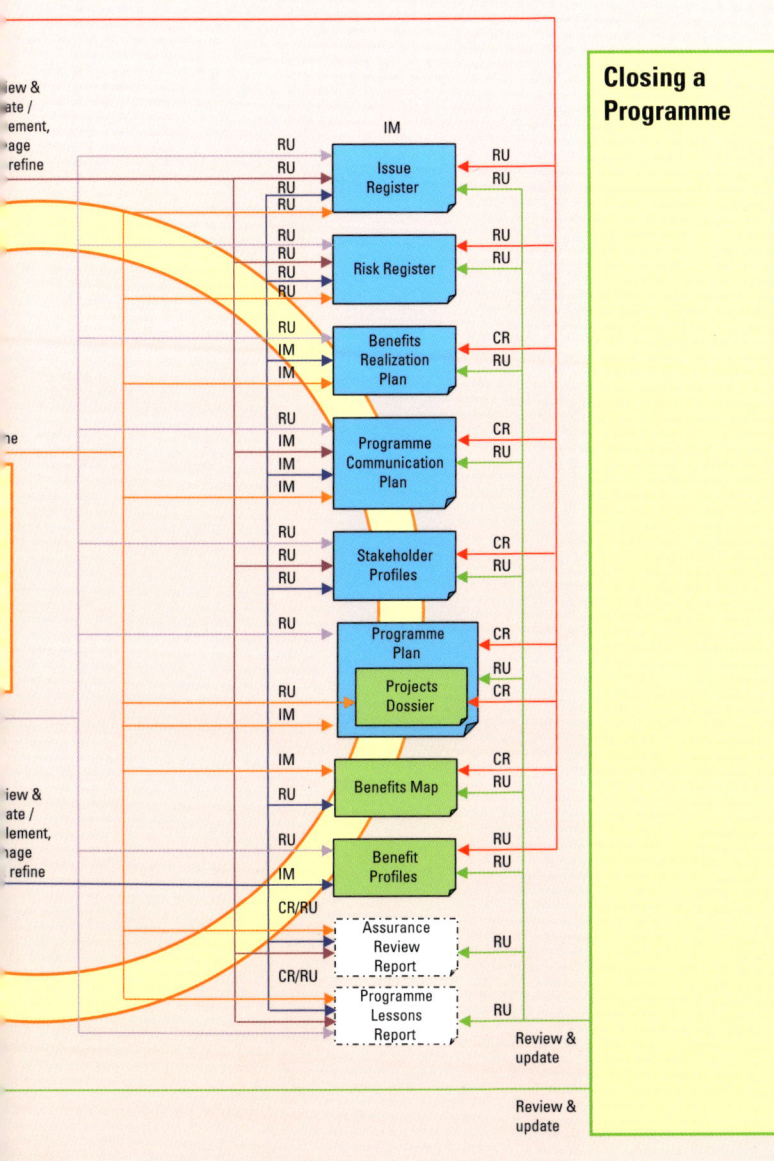

Boundary information: Those which set out the direction and the scope of the programme.

Benefit Profile /SRO/ /BCM/ /PgM/
A detailed understanding of what will be involved and how the benefit will be realised.

Benefit Map /SRO/ /BCM/ /PgM/
Illustrates the sequential relationship between benefits.

Blueprint /SRO/ /PgM/ /BCM/
Description of the required transformation and business change in terms of Processes, Organization, Technology and Information.

Business Case /SRO/ /PgM/ /BCM/
Validates the initiation of the programme and the ongoing viability of the programme.

Programme Brief /SG/ /SRO/
Shows whether the programme is viable and achievable.

Programme Definition Document /SRO/ /PgM/ /BCM/
A document that is used to consolidate or summarize the information that was used to define the programme.

Programme Mandate /SG/
Description of required outcomes from the programme, based on strategic or policy objectives.

Projects Dossier /SRO/ /PgM/ /BCM/
A list of projects required to deliver the blueprint, with high-level information and estimates.

Vision Statement /SG/ /SRO/ /BCM/
Description of the end goal of the programme; could be seen as providing an external 'artist's impression' of the desired future state.

Governance information: Those that set the standards and frameworks within which the programme will be delivered (How).

Benefits Management Strategy /SRO/ /PgM/ /BCM/
The approach to realizing benefits and the framework within which benefits realization will be achieved.

Information Management Strategy /SRO/ /PgM/ /BCM/
Description of the measures, systems and techniques that will be used to maintain and control programme information.

Issue Management Strategy /SRO/ /PgM/ /BCM/
Description of the mechanisms and procedures for resolving issues.

Monitoring and Control Strategy /SRO/ /PgM/ /BCM/
Defines how the programme will apply internal controls to itself.

Organization Structure /SRO/ /PgM/ /BCM/
Description of the management roles, responsibilities and reporting lines in the programme.

Quality and Assurance Strategy /SRO/ /PgM/ /BCM/
Description of the activities for managing quality across the programme.

Resource Management Strategy /SRO/ /PgM/ /BCM/
Description of how the programme will acquire and manage the resources required to achieve the business change.

Risk Management Strategy /SRO/ /PgM/ /BCM/
Description of the programme approach to risk management.

Stakeholder Engagement Strategy /SRO/ /PgM/ /BCM/
Description of the framework that will enable effective stakeholder engagement and communication.

Approver Producer Reviewer
/SRO/ /PgM/ /BCM/

SRO = Senior Responsible Owner
BCM = Business Change Manager
PgM = Programme Manager
SG = Sponsoring Group